Air Fryer Recipes For Beginners

Super Easy And Crispy Recipes for Smart People on a Budget. A Simple Cookbook For Air Fryer Lovers

Claire Jones

Table of Content

INTRODUCTION 9

BREAKFAST 10

    BACON AND HOT DOGS OMELET 11
    TOASTIES AND SAUSAGE IN EGG POND 12
    HEALTHY TOFU OMELET 14
    PEANUT BUTTER BANANA BREAD 16
    MILKY SCRAMBLED EGGS 18
    CHICKEN OMELET 20

MAINS 22

    CHICKEN AND CELERY STEW 23
    BROCCOLI STEW 24
    BUTTERY COD BAKE 25
    FENNEL AND TOMATO STEW 26
    TURKEY AND BOK CHOY 28
    EGGPLANT BAKE 29

SIDES 30

    MINTY PEAS 31
    LEMONY ARTICHOKES 32
    BUTTERNUT PUREE 33
    BELL PEPPER AND LETTUCE SIDE SALAD 34
    CARROT PUREE 35

SEAFOOD 36

    BEST COD EVER 37
    CRISPY SHRIMP WITH ORANGE MARMALADE DIP 39
    COD CAKES 41
    TUNA-STUFFED POTATO BOATS 43
    HONEY GLAZED SALMON 45
    HAM-WRAPPED PRAWNS WITH ROASTED PEPPER CHUTNEY 47

PUOLTRY 49

    SAUSAGE, HAM AND HASH BROWN BAKE 50
    ITALIAN TASTY CHICKEN RECIPE 52
    CREAMY MUSHROOM CHICKEN RECIPE 54
    CHICKEN BREASTS AND TOMATOES SAUCE 56

THE BEST CHICKEN BURGERS EVER 58
. CHINESE STICKY CHICKEN WINGS RECIPE 60

MEAT **63**

BASIL PORK CHOPS 63
CRISPY BRATS 64
BACON CHEESE-BURGER CASSEROLE................................... 65
SEARED RIBEYE... 67
LAMB CAKES... 69
LASAGNA CASSEROLE... 71

EGGS AND DAIRY...**73**

BROCCOLI BITES WITH CHEESE SAUCE 73

VEGETABLE **75**

CHEESY ARTICHOKES.. 75
AVOCADO AND TOMATO SALAD 76
ALMOND TOMATOES MIX 77
SESAME BROCCOLI MIX... 78

SNACK **79**

SPINACH AND ONION DIP 79
PORK BELLY BITES.. 80
ARTICHOKES DIP... 81
CRAB AND ARTICHOKE DIP 82
SPINACH ARTICHOKE DIP 84
JALAPEÑO BACON CHEESE BREAD 85
OLIVES DIP... 86
PAPRIKA TOMATOES 87
MOZZARELLA STICKS 88

DESSERT **90**

ZUCCHINI BREAD 90
ALMOND MANGO MIX 92
STRAWBERRY TART... 93
RASPBERRY MUFFINS 95
CHERRIES BREAD.. 96
COCOA AND NUTS BOMBS 97
SWEET ZUCCHINI BREAD.. 98
COCONUT.. 99
CREAM AND COCONUT CUPS... 100
AVOCADO GRANOLA.. 101
CREAMY CHIA SEEDS PUDDING 101
CINNAMON PLUMS.. 102

ORANGOE CREAM 103

CONCLUSION **105**

Introduction

Congratulations on purchasing your copy of **Air Fryer Recipes For Beginners: Super Easy And Crispy Recipes for Smart People on a Budget. A Simple Cookbook For Air Fryer Lovers**, and thank you for doing so.

I'm glad you chose to take this opportunity to welcome the air fryer diet into your life. I'm sure this book will help you find all the information and tools you need to better integrate the air fryer diet plan with your habits.

Also, I thought I'd share with you some delicious ideas and recipes for all tastes and the best of your low carb diet that I hope you'll enjoy.

You'll find hundreds of easy-to-make ideas that will best suit your situation or needs of the moment, with all the preparation times, portion sizes and a list of all the nutritional values you'll need

BREAKFAST

Bacon and Hot Dogs Omelet

Preparation Time: 10 minutes

Cooking time: 10 minutes

Servings: 2

Ingredients:

- 4 eggs

- 1 bacon slice, chopped

- 2 hot dogs, chopped

- 2 small onions, chopped

- 2 tablespoons milk

- Salt and black pepper, to taste

Directions:

1. Preheat the Air fryer to 325 o F and grease an Air Fryer pan.

2. Whisk together eggs and stir in the remaining ingredients.

3. Stir well to combine and place in the Air fryer.

4. Cook for about 10 minutes and serve hot.

Nutrition:

Calories: 418, Fat: 31.5g, Carbohydrates: 9.7g, Sugar: 5.6g, Protein: 23.4g, Sodium: 1000mg

Toasties and Sausage in Egg Pond

Preparation Time: 10 minutes Cooking time: 22 minutes Servings: 2 Ingredients:

• 3 eggs

• 2 cooked sausages, sliced

• 1 bread slice, cut into sticks

• 1/8 cup mozzarella cheese, grated

• 1/8 cup Parmesan cheese, grated

• . cup cream

Directions:

1. Preheat the Air fryer to 365 o F and grease 2 ramekins lightly.

2. Whisk together eggs with cream in a bowl and place in the ramekins.

3. Stir in the bread and sausage slices in the egg mixture and top with cheese.

4. Transfer the ramekins in the Air fryer basket and cook for about 22 minutes.

5. Dish out and serve warm.

Nutrition:

Calories: 261, Fat: 18.8g, Carbohydrates: 4.2g, Sugar: 1.3g, Protein: 18.3g, Sodium: 428mg

Healthy Tofu Omelet

Preparation Time: 10 minutes Cooking time: 29 minutes Servings: 2

Ingredients:

• . of onion, chopped

• 12-ounce silken tofu, pressed and sliced

• 3 eggs, beaten

• 1 tablespoon chives, chopped

• 1 garlic clove, minced

• 2 teaspoons olive oil

• Salt and black pepper, to taste

Directions:

1. Preheat the Air fryer to 355 0 F and grease an Air fryer pan with olive oil.

2. Add onion and garlic to the greased pan and cook for about 4 minutes.

3. Add tofu, mushrooms and chives and season with salt and black pepper.

4. Beat the eggs and pour over the tofu mixture.

5. Cook for about 25 minutes, poking the eggs twice in between.

6. Dish out and serve warm.

Nutrition:

Calories: 248, Fat: 15.9g, Carbohydrates:
6.5g, Sugar: 3.3g, Protein: 20.4g, Sodium:155mg

Peanut Butter Banana Bread

Preparation Time: 15 minutes Cooking time: 40 minutes Servings: 6

Ingredients:

- 1 cup plus 1 tablespoon all-purpose flour

- 1. teaspoons baking powder

- 1 large egg

- 2 medium ripe bananas, peeled and mashed

- . cup walnuts, roughly chopped

- . teaspoon salt

- 1/3 cup granulated sugar

- 2 tablespoons creamy peanut butter

- 2 tablespoons sour cream

- 1 teaspoon vanilla extract

Directions:

1. Preheat the Air fryer to 330 o F and grease a non-stick baking dish.

2. Mix together the flour, baking powder and salt in a bowl.

3. Whisk together egg with sugar, canola oil, sour cream, peanut butter and vanilla extract in a bowl.

4. Stir in the bananas and beat until well combined.

5. Now, add the flour mixture and fold in the walnuts gently.

6. Mix until combined and transfer the mixture evenly into the prepared baking dish.

7. Arrange the baking dish in an Air fryer basket and cook for about 40 minutes.

8. Remove from the Air fryer and place onto a wire rack to cool.

9. Cut the bread into desired size slices and serve.

Nutrition:

Calories: 384, Fat: 2.6g, Carbohydrates:

39.3g, Sugar: 16.6g, Protein: 8.9g, Sodium: 189mg

Milky Scrambled Eggs

Preparation Time: 10minutes Cooking time: 9 minutes Servings: 2

Ingredients:

• . cup milk

• 4 eggs

• 8 grape tomatoes, halved

• . cup Parmesan cheese, grated

• 1 tablespoon butter

• Salt and black pepper, to taste

Directions:

1. Preheat the Air fryer to 360 o F and grease an Air fryer pan with butter.

2. Whisk together eggs with milk, salt and black pepper in a bowl.

3. Transfer the egg mixture into the prepared pan and place in the Air fryer.

4. Cook for about 6 minutes and stir in the grape tomatoes and cheese.

5. Cook for about 3 minutes and servewarm.

Nutrition:

Calories: 351, Fat: 22g, Carbohydrates: 5.2g, Sugar: 17.7g, Protein: 26.4g, Sodium: 422mg

Chicken Omelet

Preparation Time: 15 minutes

Cooking time: 16 minutes

Servings: 8

Ingredients:

- 1 teaspoon butter

- 1 onion, chopped

- ½ jalapeño pepper, seeded and chopped

- 3 eggs

- ¼ cup chicken, cooked and shredded

- Salt and black pepper, to taste

Directions:

1. Preheat the Air fryer to 355 0 F and grease an Air Fryer pan.

2. Heat butter in a frying pan over medium heat and add onions.

3. Sauté for about 5 minutes and add jalapeño pepper.

4. Sauté for about 1 minute and stir in the chicken.

5. Remove from the heat and keep aside.

6. Meanwhile, whisk together the eggs, salt, and black pepper in a bowl.

7. Place the chicken mixture into the prepared pan and top with the egg mixture.

8. Cook for about 10 minutes until completely done and serve hot.

Nutrition:

Calories: 161, Fat: 3.4g, Carbohydrates: 5.9g, Sugar: 3g, Protein: 14.1g, Sodium: 197mg

MAINS

Chicken and Celery Stew

Preparation Time: 35 minutes

Servings: 6

Ingredients:

- 1 lb. chicken breasts, skinless; boneless and cubed

- 4 celery stalks; chopped.

- ½ cup coconut cream

- 2 red bell peppers; chopped.

- 2 tsp. garlic; minced

- 1 tbsp. butter, soft

- Salt and black pepper to taste.

Directions:

1. Grease a baking dish that fits your air fryer with the butter, add all the ingredients in the pan and toss them.

2. Introduce the dish in the fryer, cook at 360°F for 30 minutes, divide into bowls and serve

Nutrition: Calories: 246; Fat: 12g; Fiber: 2g; Carbs: 6g; Protein: 12g

Broccoli Stew

Preparation Time: 20 minutes Servings: 4 Ingredients:

• 1 broccoli head, florets separated

• . cup celery; chopped.

• . cup tomato sauce

• 3 spring onions; chopped.

• 3 tbsp. chicken stock

• Salt and black pepper to taste.

Directions:

1. In a pan that fits your air fryer, mix all the ingredients, toss, introduce the pan in your fryer and cook at 380°F for 15 minutes

2. Divide into bowls and serve for lunch.

Nutrition: Calories: 183; Fat: 4g; Fiber: 2g;

Carbs: 4g; Protein: 7g

Buttery Cod Bake

Preparation Time: 17 minutes Servings: 4

Ingredients:

• 2 cod fillets, boneless, skinless and cubed • . cup tomato sauce

• 8 cherry tomatoes; halved

• 3 tbsp. butter; melted

• 2 tbsp. parsley; chopped.

• Salt and black pepper to taste.

Directions:

1. In a baking pan that fits the air fryer, combine all the ingredients, toss, put the pan in the machine and cook the mix at 390°F for 12 minutes

2. Divide the mix into bowls and serve for lunch.

Nutrition: Calories: 232; Fat: 8g; Fiber: 2g; Carbs: 5g; Protein: 11g

Fennel and Tomato Stew

Preparation Time: 25 minutes

Servings: 4

Ingredients:

- 2 fennel bulbs; shredded

- ½ cup chicken stock

- 1 red bell pepper; chopped.

- 2 garlic cloves; minced

- 2 cups tomatoes; cubed

- 2 tbsp. tomato puree

- 1 tsp. rosemary; dried

- 1 tsp. sweet paprika

- Salt and black pepper to taste.

Directions:

1. In a pan that fits your air fryer, mix all the ingredients, toss, introduce in the fryer and cook at 380°F for 15 minutes

2. Divide the stew into bowls.

Nutrition: Calories: 184; Fat: 7g; Fiber: 2g; Carbs: 3g; Protein: 8g

Turkey and Bok Choy

Preparation Time: 25 minutes

Servings: 4

Ingredients:

- 1 turkey breast, boneless, skinless and cubed

- 2 cups bok choy; torn and steamed

- 1 tbsp. balsamic vinegar

- 2 tsp. olive oil

- ½ tsp. sweet paprika

- Salt and black pepper to taste.

Directions:

1. Take a bowl and mix the turkey with the oil, paprika, salt and pepper, toss, transfer them to your Air Fryer's basket and cook at 350°F for 20 minutes

2. In a salad, mix the turkey with all the other ingredients, toss and serve.

Nutrition: Calories: 250; Fat: 13g; Fiber: 3g; Carbs: 6g; Protein: 14g

Eggplant Bake

Preparation Time: 25 minutes

Servings: 4

Ingredients:

- ½ lb. cherry tomatoes; cubed

- ½ cup cilantro; chopped.

- 4 garlic cloves; minced

- 2 eggplants; cubed

- 1 hot chili pepper; chopped.

- 4 spring onions; chopped.

- 2 tsp. olive oil

- Salt and black pepper to taste.

Directions:

1. Grease a baking pan that fits the air fryer with the oil and mix all the ingredients in the pan.

2. Put the pan in the preheated air fryer and cook at 380°F for 20 minutes, divide into bowls and serve

Nutrition: Calories: 232; Fat: 12g; Fiber: 3g; Carbs: 5g; Protein: 10g

SIDES

Minty Peas

Preparation time: 5 minutes Cooking time: 12 minutes Servings: 4

Ingredients:

- 1 pound fresh peas

- 1 green onion, sliced

- 1 tablespoon mint, chopped

- . cup veggie stock

- 1 tablespoon butter, melted

- Salt and black pepper to taste

Directions:

1. Place all of the ingredients into a pan that fits your air fryer and mix well.

2. Put the pan in the air fryer and cook at 370 degrees F for 12 minutes.

3. Divide between plates and serve.

Nutrition: calories 151, fat 2, fiber 6, carbs 9, protein 5

Lemony Artichokes

Preparation time: 10 minutes Cooking time: 25 minutes Servings: 4

Ingredients:

• 2 medium artichokes, trimmed

• Juice of . lemon

• A drizzle of olive oil

• Salt to taste

Directions:

1. Brush the artichokes with the oil, season with salt, and put them in your air fryer's basket.

2. Cook at 370 degrees F for 20 minutes.

3. Divide between plates, drizzle lemon juice all over, and serve.

Nutrition: calories 151, fat 3, fiber 7, carbs 8, protein 4

Butternut Puree

Preparation time: 5 minutes   Cooking time: 20 minutes
Servings: 4

Ingredients:

• 1 cup veggie stock

• 1 butternut squash, peeled and cut

into medium chunks

• 2 tablespoons butter, melted

• 1 yellow onion, thinly sliced

• . teaspoon apple pie spice

• Salt and black pepper to taste

Directions:

1. In a pan that fits your air fryer, mix the stock, squash, onion, spice, salt, and pepper; stir well.

2. Place the pan in the fryer and cook at 370 degrees F for 20 minutes.

3. Transfer the squash mixture to a blender, add the butter, and pulse well.

4. Divide between plates and serve as a side dish.

Nutrition: calories 200, fat 6, fiber 7, carbs 15, protein 5

Bell Pepper and Lettuce Side Salad

Preparation time: 5 minutes Cooking time: 15 minutes Servings: 4

Ingredients:

• 1 tablespoon lemon juice

• 1 red bell pepper

• 1 lettuce head, torn

• Salt and black pepper to taste

• 3 tablespoons yogurt

• 2 tablespoons olive oil

Directions:

1. In your air fryer, place the bell pepper along with the oil, salt, and pepper; air

fry at 400 degrees F for 15 minutes. 2. Cool the bell pepper down, peel, cut it into strips and put it in a bowl.

3. Add lettuce, lemon juice, yogurt, salt, and pepper.

4. Toss well, and serve as a side dish.

Nutrition: calories 150, fat 1, fiber 3, carbs 3, protein 2

Carrot Puree

Preparation time: 10 minutes Cooking time: 15 minutes Servings: 4

Ingredients:

• 1. pounds carrots, peeled and chopped

• 1 tablespoon butter, softened

• Salt and black pepper to taste

• 1 cup chicken stock, heated up

• 1 tablespoon honey

• 1 teaspoon brown sugar

Directions:

1. In a pan that fits your air fryer, mix the carrots with the stock, salt, pepper, and sugar; stir well.

2. Put the pan into the fryer and cook at 370 degrees F for 15 minutes.

3. Transfer the carrot mixture to a blender, add the butter and the honey, and pulse well.

4. Divide between plates and serve.

Nutrition: calories 100, fat 3, fiber 3, carbs 7, protein 6

SEAFOOD

Best Cod Ever

Preparation Time: 15 minutes

Cooking time: 7 minutes

Servings: 2

Ingredients:

• 2, 4-ounceskinless codfish fillets, cut

into rectangular pieces

• . cup flour

• 3 eggs

• 1 green chili, chopped finely

• 3 scallions, chopped finely

• 2 garlic cloves, minced

• 1 teaspoon light soy sauce

• Salt and black pepper, to taste

Directions:

1. Preheat the Air fryer to 375 o F and

grease an Air fryer basket.

2. Place the flour in a shallow dish and

mix remaining ingredients in another

shallow dish except cod.

3. Coat each fillet with the flour and then dip into the egg mixture.

4. Place the cod in the Air fryer basket and cook for about 7 minutes.

5. Dish out in a platter and serve warm.

Nutrition:

Calories: 405, Fat: 8.4g, Carbohydrates: 28.2g, Sugar: 1.7g, Protein: 51.1g, Sodium:439mg

Crispy Shrimp with Orange Marmalade Dip

Preparation Time: 25minutes Cooking time: 20 minutes Servings: 4

Ingredients:

• 8 large shrimp, peeled and deveined

• 8 ounces coconut milk

• . cup panko breadcrumbs

• Salt and black pepper, to taste

• . teaspoon cayenne pepper

For Dip:

• . cup orange marmalade

• 1 teaspoon mustard

• . teaspoon hot sauce

• 1 tablespoon honey

Directions:

1. Preheat the Air fryer to 350 o F and grease an Air fryer basket.

2. Mix coconut milk, salt and black pepper in a shallow dish.

3. Combine breadcrumbs, cayenne pepper, salt and black pepper in another shallow dish.

4. Coat the shrimps in coconut milk mixture and then roll into the breadcrumb mixture.

5. Arrange the shrimps in the Air fryer basket and cook for about 20 minutes.

6. Meanwhile, mix all the dip ingredients and serve with shrimp.

Nutrition:

Calories: 316, Fat: 14.7g, Carbohydrates:

44.3g, Sugar: 31.1g, Protein: 6g, Sodium:

165mg

Cod Cakes

Preparation Time: 15 minutes Cooking time: 14 minutes Servings: 4

Ingredients:

• 1 pound cod fillets

• 1 egg

• 1/3 cup coconut, grated and divided

• 1 scallion, chopped finely

• 2 tablespoons fresh parsley, chopped

• 1 teaspoon fresh lime zest, grated finely

• 1 teaspoon red chili paste

• Salt, to taste

• 1 tablespoon fresh lime juice

Directions:

1. Preheat the Air fryer to 375 0 F and grease an Air fryer basket.

2. Put cod filets, lime zest, egg, chili paste, salt and lime juice in a food processor and pulse until smooth.

3. Transfer the cod mixture to a bowl and add 2 tablespoons coconut, scallion and parsley.

4. Make 12 equal sized round cakes from the mixture.

5. Put the remaining coconut in a shallow dish and coat the cod cakes in it.

6. Arrange 6 cakes in the Air fryer basket and cook for about 7 minutes. serve warm.

Nutrition: Calories: 171, Fat: 3.3g, Carbohydrates: 16.1g, Sugar: 13.2g, Protein: 19g, Sodium: 115mg

Tuna-Stuffed Potato Boats

Cooking time: 16 minutes Servings: 4 Ingredients:

• 4 starchy potatoes, soaked for about 30 minutes and drain

• 1, 6-ouncecan tuna, drained

• 2 tablespoons plain Greek yogurt

• 1 scallion, chopped and divided

• 1 tablespoon capers

• . tablespoon olive oil

• 1 teaspoon red chili powder

• Salt and black pepper, to taste

Directions:

1. Preheat the Air fryer to 355 o F and grease an Air fryer basket.

2. Arrange the potatoes in the Air fryer basket and cook for about 30 minutes.

3. Meanwhile, mix tuna, yogurt, red chili powder, salt, black pepper and half of scallion in a bowl and mash the mixture well.

4. Remove the potatoes from the Air fryer and halve the potatoes lengthwise carefully.

5. Stuff in the tuna mixture in the potatoes and top with capers and

remaining scallion.

6. Dish out in a platter and serve immediately.

Nutrition:

Calories: 281, Fat: 13g, Carbohydrates: 15.4g, Sugar: 1.8g,Protein: 26.2g, Sodium: 249mg

Honey Glazed Salmon

Preparation Time: 10 minutes

Cooking time: 14 minutes

Servings: 2

Ingredients:

- 1 teaspoon water

- 2, 3½-ouncesalmon fillets

- 1/3 cup soy sauce

- 1/3 cup honey

- 3 teaspoons rice wine vinegar

Directions:

1. Preheat the Air fryer to 355 0 F and grease an Air fryer grill pan.

2. Mix all the ingredients in a small bowl except salmon.

3. Reserve half of the mixture in a small bowl and coat the salmon in remaining mixture.

4. Refrigerate, covered for about 2 hours and place the salmon in the Air fryer grill pan.

5. Cook for about 13 minutes, flipping once in between and coat with reserved marinade.

6. Place the reserved marinade in a small pan and cook for about 1 minute.

7. Serve salmon with marinade sauce and enjoy.

Nutrition: Calories: 331, Fat: 6.1g, Carbohydrates: 49.8g, Sugar: 47.1g, Protein: 22.1g, Sodium: 2442mg

Ham-Wrapped Prawns with Roasted Pepper Chutney

Preparation Time: 15minute s Cooking time: 13 minutes Servings: 4

Ingredients:

• 1 large red bell pepper

• 8 king prawns, peeled and deveined

• 4 ham slices, halved

• 1 garlic clove, minced

• 1 tablespoon olive oil

• . tablespoon paprika

• Salt and freshly ground black pepper, to taste

Directions:

1. Preheat the Air fryer to 375 o Fand grease an Air fryer basket.

2. Place the bell pepper in the Air fryer basket and cook forabout 10 minutes.

3. Dish out the bell pepper into a bowl and keep aside, covered for about 15 minutes.

4. Now, peel the bell pepper and remove the stems and seeds and chop it.

5. Put the chopped bell pepper, garlic, paprika and olive oil in a blender and pulse until a puree is formed.

6. Wrap each ham slice around each prawn and transfer to the Air fryer basket.

7. Cook for about 3 minutes and serve with roasted pepper chutney.

Nutrition:

Calories: 353, Fat: 9.9g, Carbohydrates:7.6g, Sugar: 1.8g, Protein: 55.4g, Sodium: 904mg

PUOLTRY

Sausage, Ham and Hash Brown Bake

Preparation Time: 45 minutes

Servings: 4

Nutrition: 509 Calories; 20.1g Fat; 40g Carbs; 41.2g Protein; 3.9g Sugars

Ingredients

- 1/2 pound chicken sausages, smoked

- ☐ 1/2 pound ham, sliced

- 6 ounces hash browns, frozen and shredded

- 2 garlic cloves, minced

- 8 ounces spinach

- 1/2 cup Ricotta cheese

- 1/2 cup Asiago cheese, grated

- 4 eggs

- 1/2 cup yogurt

- 1/2 cup milk

- Salt and ground black pepper, to taste

- 1 teaspoon smoked paprika

Directions

1. Start by preheating your Air Fryer to 380 degrees F. Cook the sausages and ham for 10 minutes; set aside.

2. Meanwhile, in a preheated saucepan, cook the hash browns and garlic for 4 minutes, stirring frequently; remove from the heat, add the spinach and cover with the lid.

3. Allow the spinach to wilt completely. Transfer the sautéed mixture to a baking pan. Add the reserved sausage and ham.

4. In a mixing dish, thoroughly combine the cheese, eggs, yogurt, milk, salt, pepper, and paprika. Pour the cheese mixture over the hash browns in the pan.

5. Place the baking pan in the cooking basket and cook approximately 30 minutes or until everything is thoroughly cooked. Bon appétit!

Italian Tasty Chicken Recipe

Preparation Time: 26 Minutes Servings: 4

Ingredients:

• chicken thighs-5

• olive oil-1 tbsp.

• grated parmesan-1/4 cup

• sun dried tomatoes-1/2 cup

• minced garlic cloves-2

• chopped thyme -1 tbsp.

• heavy cream-1/2 cup

• chicken stock-3/4 cup

• crushed red pepper flakes-1 tsp.

• chopped basil-2 tbsp.

• Salt and black pepper to the taste

Directions:

1. Start by spicing the chicken with saltand pepper, rub the majority of the spiced chicken with half of the oil

2. Preheat your air fryer to a temperatureof 350 °F and acquaint your chicken atthat point permit with cook for 4 minutes.

3. On the other hand; heat a container with the remainder of the oil to over medium- high temperature, in this way present thyme garlic, pepper pieces, sundried tomatoes, overwhelming cream,stock, parmesan, salt, and pepper; at that point, blend appropriately and bring to a stew.

4. Remove container with the blend from the cooking heat and move to a dish that accommodates your air fryer.

5. Include chicken thighs over the dishnd move into your air fryer and cookat 320

°F, for 12 minutes.6. Serve the supper with basil sprinkledon top.

Nutrition:

Calories: 272; Fat: 9; Fiber: 12; Protein:23;Carbs:37;

Creamy Mushroom Chicken Recipe

Preparation Time: 40 Minutes Servings: 8

Ingredients:

• Dried thyme-1/2 tsp.

• Dried basil; -1/2 tsp.

• chicken thighs-8

• Dried oregano-1/2 tsp.

• Grated parmesan-1/4 cup

• halved cremini mushrooms; -8 oz.

• mustard-1 tbsp.

• minced cloves; -3 garlic

• chicken stock-1 cup

• Melted butter-3 tbsp.

• heavy cream-1/4 cup

• Salt and black pepper to the taste

Directions:

1. Rub chicken pieces with 2 tbsp. spread, flavor with salt and pepper at that point put in your air fryer's crate, cook at 370 °F, for 5 minutes and leave aside in a bowl until further notice.

2. On the other hand; heat a dish with the remainder of the spread to over medium- high warmth, present mushrooms and garlic; mix and cook

for 5 minutes.

3. Include salt, pepper, stock, oregano,thyme, and basil; blend appropriately move to an protected dish that accommodates your air fryer.

4. Include chicken and join everything, put in your air fryer and cook at 370 °F, for20 minutes.

5. Include parmesan, substantial cream, and mustard remix everything, cook for 5 minutes more,

6. Share meal among plates and serve. Nutrition: Calories: 34

Chicken Breasts and Tomatoes Sauce

Preparation Time: 30

Minutes Servings: 4

Ingredients:

• skinless and boneless chicken breasts-4

• balsamic vinegar-1/4 cup

• chopped red onion -1

• Grated parmesan-1/4 cup.

• Chopped canned tomatoes-14 oz.

• garlic powder-1/4 tsp

• Salt and black pepper to the taste

• Cooking spray

Directions:

1. Start by Spraying a heating dish that accommodates your air fryer with cooking oil, include chicken, seasonwith s alt, pepper, balsamic vinegar, garlic powder, tomatoes and cheddar and blend everything appropriately,

2. Introduce the chicken into your air fryer and cook at 400 °F, for 20 minutes.

3. Share feast among plates and serve hot.

Nutrition:

Calories: 250; Fat: 12; Fiber: 12; Carbs: 19; Protein: 28

The Best Chicken Burgers Ever

Preparation Time: 20 minutes

Servings: 4

Nutrition: 507 Calories; 26.5g Fat; 37.6g Carbs; 30g Protein; 12.8g Sugars

Ingredients

- 1 tablespoon olive oil

- 1 onion, peeled and finely chopped

- 2 garlic cloves, minced

- Sea salt and ground black pepper, to taste

- 1/2 teaspoon paprika

- 1/2 teaspoon ground cumin

- 1 pound chicken breast, ground

- 4 soft rolls

- 4 tablespoons ketchup

- 4 tablespoons mayonnaise

- 2 teaspoons Dijon mustard

- 4 tablespoons green onions, chopped

- 4 pickles, sliced

Directions

1. Heat the olive oil in a skillet over high flame. Then, sauté the onion until golden and translucent, about 4 minutes.

2. Add the garlic and cook an additional 30 seconds or until it is aromatic. Season with salt, pepper, paprika, and cumin; reserve.

3. Add the chicken and cook for 2 to 3 minutes, stirring and crumbling with a fork. Add the onion mixture and mix to combine well.

4. Shape the mixture into patties and transfer them to the cooking basket. Cook in the preheated Air Fryer at 360 degrees F for 6 minutes. Turn them over and cook an additional 5 minutes. Work in batches.

5. Smear the base of the roll with ketchup, mayo, and mustard. Top with the chicken, green onions, and pickles. Enjoy!

. Chinese Sticky Chicken Wings Recipe

Preparation Time: 2 hours 15 Minutes Servings: 6

Ingredients:

• Honey-2 tbsp.

• Salt and black pepper to the taste

• white pepper-1/4 tsp.

• Soy sauce-2 tbsp.

• Lime juice-3 tbsp.

• chicken wings-16

Directions:

1. Combine honey with soy sauce, salt, highly contrasting pepper, and lime juice, whisk well, include chicken pieces, hurl to coat in a bowl

2. Refrigerate for 2 hours.

3. Move the whole blend to your air fryer, and cook at 370 °F, for 6 minutes on each side; increment warmth to 400 °F and cook for an additional 3 minutes.

4. Serve hot.

Nutrition:

Calories: 372; Fat: 9; Fiber: 10; Protein: 24;Carbs: 37

Creamy Chicken and Rice with Peas

Preparation Time: 40 Minutes Servings: 4

Ingredients:

• Chicken breasts; skinless,boneless and cut into quarters-1lb.

• chicken stock-1 cup

• already cooked white rice-1 cup

• chopped parsley- 1/4 cup

• frozen peas-2 cups

• parmesan; grated-1 . cups

• minced garlic cloves; -3

• Olive oil-1 tbsp.

• chopped yellow onion-1

• heavy cream-1/4 cup

• white wine-1/2 cup

• Salt and black pepper to the taste

Directions:

1. Spice your chicken bosoms with salt and pepper, at that point gradually pour half of the oil over them, rub well and put in your air fryer's container and cook them at 360 °F, for 6 minutes.

2. Heat a skillet with the remainder of the oil over medium-high warmth, include garlic, onion, wine, stock, salt, pepper, and substantial cream; blend, bring to a stew and cook for 9 minutes.

3. Move chicken bosoms to a heatproof dish that accommodates your air fryer, Include peas, rice and cream blend over them, hurl, sprinkle parmesan and parsley everywhere,

4. Introduce blend into your air fryer and cook at 420 °F, for 10 minutes.

5. Serve bosom and rice among plates hot.

Nutrition:

Calories: 313; Fat: 12; Fiber: 14; Carbs: 27; Protein: 44

MEAT

Basil Pork Chops

Preparation Time: 30 minutes Servings: 4

Ingredients:

- 4 pork chops

- 2 tsp. basil; dried

- . tsp. chili powder

- 2 tbsp. olive oil

- A pinch of salt and black pepper

Directions:

1. In a pan that fits your air fryer, mixall the ingredients, toss.

2. Introduce in the fryer and cook at 400°F for 25 minutes. Divide everythingbetween plates and serve

Nutrition: Calories: 274; Fat: 13g; Fiber: 4g;Carbs: 6g; Protein: 18g

Crispy Brats

Preparation Time: 20minutes Servings: 4Ingredients:

• 4, 3-oz.beef bratwursts

Directions:

1. Place brats into the air fryer basket.

2. Adjust the temperature to 375 Degrees F and set the timer for 15 minutes.

Nutrition: Calories: 286; Protein: 11.8g;Fiber: 0.0g; Fat: 24.8g; Carbs: 0.0g

Bacon Cheese-burger Casserole

Preparation Time: 35 minutes Servings: 4

Ingredients:

• 1 lb. 80/20 ground beef.

• 4 slices sugar-free bacon; cooked

and crumbled

• 1 large egg.

• 2 pickle spears; chopped

• . medium white onion; peeled. And

chopped

• 1 cup shredded Cheddar cheese, divided.

Directions:

1. Brown the ground beef in a medium skillet over medium heat about 7– 10minutes. When no pink remains, drainthe fat. Remove from heat and add ground beef to large mixing bowl.

2. Add onion, . cup Cheddar and egg to bowl. Mix ingredients well and add crumbled bacon

3. Pour the mixture into a 4-cup roundbaking dish and top with remaining Cheddar. Place into the air fryer basket. Adjust the temperature to 375 Degrees F and set the timer for 20 minutes

4. Casserole will be golden on top and firm in the middle when fully cooked. Serve immediately with chopped pickles on top.

Nutrition: Calories: 369; Protein: 31.0g; Fiber:

0.2g; Fat: 22.6g; Carbs: 1.2g

Seared Ribeye

Preparation Time: 50 minutes Servings: 2

Ingredients:

- 1, 8-oz.ribeye steak

- 1 tbsp. salted butter; softened.

- 1 tbsp. coconut oil

- . tsp. dried parsley.

- . tsp. pink Himalayan salt

- . tsp. ground peppercorn

- . tsp. dried oregano.

- . tsp. garlic powder.

Directions:

1. Rub steak with salt and ground peppercorn. Place into the air fryer basket.

2. Adjust the temperature to 250 Degrees F and set the timer for 45 minutes.

3. After timer beeps, begin checking doneness and add a few minutes until internal temperature is your personal preference

4. In a medium skillet over medium heat, add coconut oil. When oil is hot,quickly sear outside and sides of steak until crisp and browned. Remove from heat and allow steak to rest

5. In a small bowl, whip butter with garlic powder, parsley and oregano. Slice steak and serve with herb butter on top.

Nutrition: Calories: 377; Protein:

Lamb Cakes

Preparation Time: 35 minutes Servings: 8

Ingredients:

• 2 . lb. lamb meat, ground

• 2 spring onions; chopped

• . cup almond meal

• 3 eggs, whisked

• 1 tbsp. garlic; minced

• 2 tbsp. cilantro; chopped

• Zest of 1 lemon

• Juice of 1 lemon

• Cooking spray

• 2 tbsp. mint; chopped

• A pinch of salt and black pepper

Directions:

1. Take a bowl and mix all the ingredients except the cooking spray, stir well and shape medium cakes out of this mix

2. Put the cakes in your air fryer, grease them with cooking spray and cook at 390°F for 15 minutes on each side 3. Divide between plates and serve with a side salad

Nutrition: Calories: 283; Fat: 13g; Fiber: 4g; Carbs: 6g; Protein: 15g

Lasagna Casserole

Preparation Time: 30 minutes Servings: 4

Ingredients:

- . cup low-carb no-sugar-added pasta sauce

- 1 lb. 80/20 ground beef; cooke and drained

- . cup full-fat ricotta cheese

- . cup grated Parmesan cheese.

- . tsp. garlic powder.

- 1 tsp. dried parsley.

- . tsp. dried oregano.

- 1 cup shredded mozzarella cheese

Directions:

1. In a 4-cup round baking dish, pour . cup pasta sauce on the bottom of the dish. Place . of the ground beef on top of the sauce.

2. In a small bowl, mix ricotta, Parmesan, garlic powder, parsley and oregano. Place dollops of half the mixture on top of the beef

3. Sprinkle with ⅓ of the mozzarella. Repeat layers until all beef, ricotta mixture, sauce and mozzarella are used, ending with the mozzarella on top

4. Cover dish with foil and place into the air fryer basket. Adjust the temperature to 370 Degrees F and set the timer for 15 minutes. In the last 2 minutes of cooking, remove the foil to brown the cheese. Serve immediately.

Nutrition: Calories: 371; Protein: 31.4g; Fiber: 1.6g; Fat: 21.4g; Carbs: 5.8g

Broccoli Bites with Cheese Sauce

Preparation Time: 20 minutes Servings: 6

7.2g Protein; 3.6g Sugars; 3.3g Fiber

Ingredients

For the Broccoli Bites:

- 1 medium-sized head broccoli, broken into florets

- 1/2 teaspoon lemon zest, freshly grated

- 1/3 teaspoon fine sea salt

- 1/2 teaspoon hot paprika

- 1 teaspoon shallot powder

- 1 teaspoon porcini powder

- 1/2 teaspoon granulated garlic

- 1/3 teaspoon celery seeds

- 1 . tablespoons olive oil

For the Cheese Sauce:

- 2 tablespoons butter

- 1 tablespoon golden flaxseed meal

- 1 cup milk

- 1/2 cup blue cheese

Directions

1. Toss all the ingredients for the broccoli bites in a mixing bowl, covering the broccoli florets on all sides.

2. Cook them in the preheated Air Fryer at 360 degrees for 13 to 15 minutes.

3. In the meantime, melt the butter over a medium heat; stir in the golden flaxseed meal and let cook for 1 min or so.

4. Gradually pour in the milk, stirring constantly, until the mixture is smooth. Bring it to a simmer and stir in the cheese. Cook until the sauce has thickened slightly.

5. Pause your Air Fryer, mix the broccoli with the prepared sauce and

cook for further 3 minutes. Bon appétit!

VEGETABLE

Cheesy Artichokes

Preparation time: 10 minutes Cooking time: 14 minutes Servings: 4

Ingredients:

- 4 artichokes, trimmed and halved
- 1 cup cheddar cheese, shredded
- 2 tablespoons olive oil
- A pinch of salt and black pepper
- 3 garlic cloves, minced
- 1 teaspoon garlic powder

Directions:

1. In your air fryer's basket, combine the artichokes with the oil, cheese and the other ingredients, toss and cook at 400 degrees F for 14 minutes.

2. Divide everything between plates and serve.

Avocado and Tomato Salad

Preparation time: 10minutes Cooking time: 12 minutes Servings: 4

Ingredients:

• 1 pound tomatoes, cut into wedges

• 2 avocados, peeled, pitted and sliced

• 2 tablespoons avocado oil

• 1 red onion, sliced

• 1 tablespoon balsamic vinegar

• Salt and black pepper to the taste

• 1 tablespoon cilantro, chopped

Directions:

1. In your air fryer, combine the tomatoes with the avocados and the other ingredients, toss and cook at 360 degrees F for 12 minutes.

2. Divide between plates and serve.

Nutrition: calories 144, fat 7, fiber 5, carbs 8, protein 6

Almond Tomatoes Mix

Preparation time: 5 minutes Cooking time: 15 minutes Servings: 4

Ingredients:

- 1 pound cherry tomatoes, halved

- 2 tablespoons almonds, chopped

- 2 tablespoons olive oil

- 1 tablespoon balsamic vinegar

- Salt and black pepper to the taste

- . cup scallions, chopped

- 1 tablespoon chives, chopped

Directions:

1. In your air fryer, combine the tomatoes with the almonds, oil and the other ingredients, toss and cook at 380 degrees F for 15 minutes.

2. Divide everything between plates and serve.

Nutrition: calories 111, fat 4, fiber 4, carbs 9, protein 2

Sesame Broccoli Mix

Preparation time: 5 minutes Cooking time: 14 minutes Servings: 4

Ingredients:

• 1 pound broccoli florets

• 1 tablespoon sesame oil

• 1 teaspoon sesame seeds, toasted

• 1 red onion, sliced

• 1 tablespoon lime juice

• 1 teaspoon chili powder

• Salt and black pepper to the taste

Directions:

1. In your air fryer, combine the broccoli with the oil, sesame seeds and the other ingredients, toss and cook at 380 degrees F for 14 minutes.

2. Divide between plates and serve.

Nutrition: calories 141, fat 3, fiber 4, carbs 4, protein 2

SNACK

Spinach and Onion Dip

Preparation Time: 25 minutes

Servings: 6

Ingredients:

- 1 lb. spinach; torn

- 1 cup mozzarella; shredded

- 1 cup coconut cream

- 4 spring onions; chopped.

- 6 tbsp. ghee; melted

- Salt and black pepper to taste.

Directions:

1. In a pan that fits the air fryer, combine all the ingredients and whisk them really well.

2. Introduce the pan in your air fryer and cook at 370°F for 20 minutes. Divide into bowls and serve

Nutrition: Calories: 184; Fat: 12g; Fiber: 2g; Carbs: 3g; Protein: 9g

Pork Belly Bites

Preparation Time: 35 minutes Servings: 6

Ingredients:

• 2 lb. pork belly; cut into strips

• 2 tbsp. olive oil

• A pinch of salt and black pepper

• A pinch of basil; dried

• 2 tsp. fennel seeds

Directions:

1. Take a bowl and mix all the ingredients, toss and put the pork strips in your air fryer's basket and cook at 425°F for 25 minutes

2. Divide into bowls and serve as a snack.

Nutrition: Calories: 251; Fat: 14g; Fiber: 3g; Carbs: 5g; Protein: 18g

Artichokes Dip

Preparation Time: 30 minutes

Servings: 6

Ingredients:

- 2 garlic cloves; minced

- 6 oz. cream cheese, soft

- ½ cup almond milk

- 2 spring onions; minced

- 20 oz. canned artichoke hearts, drained and chopped.

- 1 cup mozzarella; shredded

- 2 tsp. olive oil

- A pinch of salt and black pepper

Directions:

1. Grease a baking pan that fits the air fryer with the oil and mix all the ingredients except the mozzarella inside.

2. Sprinkle the cheese all over, introduce the pan in the air fryer and cook at 370°F for 25 minutes

3. Divide into bowls and serve as a party dip

Nutrition: Calories: 231; Fat: 11g; Fiber: 2g; Carbs: 4g; Protein: 8g

Crab and Artichoke Dip

Preparation Time: 25 minutes Servings: 4

Ingredients:

• 8 oz. cream cheese, soft

• 12 oz. jumbo crab meat

• 1 bunch green onions; minced

• 14 oz. canned artichoke hearts, drained and chopped.

• 1 cup coconut cream

• 1 . cups mozzarella; shredded

• 1 tbsp. lemon juice

• 1 tbsp. lemon juice

• A pinch of salt and black pepper

Directions:

1. In a bowl, combine all the ingredients except half of the cheese and whisk them really well.

2. Transfer this to a pan that fits your air fryer, introduce in the machine and cook at 400°F for 15 minutes

3. Sprinkle the rest of the mozzarella on top and cook for 5 minutes more. Divide the mix into bowls and serve as a party dip

Nutrition: Calories: 240; Fat: 8g; Fiber: 2g; Carbs: 4g; Protein: 14g

Spinach Artichoke Dip

Preparation Time: 20 minutes

Servings: 6

Ingredients:

- 10 oz. frozen spinach, drained and thawed

- 8 oz. full-fat cream cheese; softened.

- 1, 14-oz.can artichoke hearts, drained and chopped

- ¼ cup chopped pickled jalapeños.

- ¼ cup full-fat mayonnaise

- ¼ cup full-fat sour cream.

- ¼ cup grated Parmesan cheese.

- 1 cup shredded pepper jack cheese

- ½ tsp. garlic powder.

Directions:

1. Mix all ingredients in a 4-cup baking bowl. Place into the air fryer basket.

2. Adjust the temperature to 320 Degrees F and set the timer for 10 minutes. Remove when brown and bubbling. Serve warm.

Nutrition: Calories: 226; Protein: 10.0g; Fiber: 3.7g; Fat: 15.9g; Carbs: 10.2g

Jalapeño Bacon Cheese Bread

Preparation Time: 25 minutes Servings: 8 sticks

Ingredients:

• 4 slices sugar-free bacon; cooked and chopped

• 2 large eggs.

• . cup chopped pickled jalapeños.

• . cup grated Parmesan cheese.

• 2 cups shredded mozzarella cheese

Directions:

1. Mix all ingredients in a large bowl. Cut a piece of parchment to fit your air fryer basket.

2. Dampen your hands with a bit of water and press out the mixture into a circle. You may need to separate this into two smaller cheese breads, depending on the size of your fryer

3. Place the parchment and cheese bread into the air fryer basket

4. Adjust the temperature to 320 Degrees F and set the timer for 15 minutes. Carefully flip the bread when 5 minutes remain

5. When fully cooked, the top will be golden brown. Serve warm.

Nutrition: Calories: 273; Protein: 20.1g; Fiber:

0.1g; Fat: 18.1g; Carbs: 2.3g

Olives Dip

Preparation Time: 10 minutes Servings: 6

Ingredients:

• 1 cup black olives, pitted and chopped.

• . cup capers

• . cup olive oil

• 1 cup parsley leaves

• 1 cup basil leaves

• 2 garlic cloves; minced

• 3 tbsp. lemon juice

• 2 tsp. apple cider vinegar

• A pinch of salt and black pepper

Directions:

1. In a blender, combine all the ingredients, pulse well and transfer to a ramekin.

2. Place the ramekin in your air fryer's basket and cook at 350°F for 5 minutes

Nutrition: Calories: 120

Paprika Tomatoes

Preparation time: 10 minutes Cooking time: 15 minutes Servings: 4

Ingredients:

• 1 pound cherry tomatoes, halved

• 1 tablespoon sweet paprika

• 2 tablespoons olive oil

• 2 garlic cloves, minced

• 1 tablespoon lime juice

• 1 tablespoon chives, chopped

Directions:

1. In your air fryer's basket, combine the tomatoes with the paprika and the other ingredients, toss and cook at 370 degrees F for 15 minutes.

2. Divide between plates and serve.

Nutrition: calories 131, fat 4, fiber 7, carbs 10, protein 8

Mozzarella Sticks

Preparation Time: 1 hour 10 minutes Servings: 12 sticks

Ingredients:

• 6, 1-oz.mozzarella string cheese sticks

• . oz. pork rinds, finely ground

• 2 large eggs.

• . cup grated Parmesan cheese.

• 1 tsp. dried parsley.

Directions:

1. Place mozzarella sticks on a cutting board and cut in half. Freeze 45 minutes or until firm. If freezing overnight, remove frozen sticks after 1 hour and place into airtight zip-top storage bag and place back in freezer for future use.

2. Take a large bowl, mix Parmesan, ground pork rinds and parsley

3. Take a medium bowl, whisk eggs

4. Dip a frozen mozzarella stick into beaten eggs and then into Parmesan mixture to coat.

5. Repeat with remaining sticks. Place mozzarella sticks into the air fryer basket.

6. Adjust the temperature to 400 Degrees F and set the timer for 10 minutes or until golden. Serve warm.

Nutrition: Calories: 236; Protein: 19.2g; Fiber:

0.0g; Fat: 13.8g; Carbs: 4.7g

DESSERT

Zucchini Bread

Preparation time: 10 minutes

Cooking time: 40 minutes

Servings: 6

Ingredients:

- ¾ cup sugar

- ½ cup butter

- 1 teaspoon almond extract

- 1 teaspoon baking soda

- 2 eggs, whisked

- 3 zucchinis, grated

- 2 cups almond flour

- 1/3 cup milk

- Cooking spray

Directions:

1. In a bowl, combine the sugar with the butter, almond extract and the other ingredients, whisk, pour into a lined loaf pan, place the pan in the air fryer and cook at 320 degrees F for 40 minutes

2. Cool down, slice and serve.

Nutrition: calories 222, fat 7, fiber 8, carbs 14, protein 4

Almond Mango Mix

Preparation time: 10 minutes

Cooking time: 12 minutes

Servings: 4

Ingredients:

- 2 teaspoons almond extract

- 3 mangoes, peeled and roughly cubed

- ½ teaspoon nutmeg powder

- 4 tablespoons butter

- 2 tablespoons brown sugar

Directions:

1. In your air fryer, combine the mangoes with the almonds extract and the other ingredients, toss and cook 360 degrees F for 12 minutes.

2. Divide into cups and serve.

Nutrition: calories 180, fat 6, fiber 8, carbs 19, protein 12

Strawberry Tart

Preparation Time: 25 minutes Servings: 8

Ingredients:

- 1 . cups almond flour

- 1/3 cup butter; melted

- 2 cups strawberries; sliced

- 5 egg whites

- 1/3 cup swerve

- Zest of 1 lemon, grated

- 1 tsp. baking powder

- 1 tsp. vanilla extract

- Cooking spray

Directions:

1. In a bowl, whisk egg whites well. Add the rest of the ingredients except the cooking spray gradually and whisk everything.

2. Grease a tart pan with the cooking spray and pour the strawberries mix

3. Put the pan in the air fryer and cook at 370°F for 20 minutes. Cool down, slice and serve

Nutrition: Calories: 182; Fat: 12g; Fiber: 1g; Carbs: 6g; Protein: 5g

Raspberry Muffins

Preparation Time: 30 minutes Servings: 8

Ingredients:

- . cup raspberries
- . cup swerve
- . cup coconut flour
- . cup ghee; melted
- 1 egg
- 3 tbsp. cream cheese
- 2 tbsp. almond meal
- . tsp. baking soda
- . tsp. baking powder
- 1 tsp. cinnamon powder
- Cookingspray

Directions:

1. Take a bowl and mix all the except the cooking spray and whisk well.

2. Grease a muffin pan that fits the air fryer with the cooking spray 3. Pour the raspberry mix, put the pan in the machine and cook at 350°F for 20 minutes. Serve the muffins cold

Nutrition: Calories: 223; Fat: 7g;

Cherries Bread

Preparation time: 10 minutes

Cooking time: 35 minutes

Servings: 4

Ingredients:

- 2 cups cherries, pitted and chopped

- 1 cup sugar

- 2 teaspoons vanilla extract

- 2 eggs, whisked

- 2 cups almond flour

- 1 tablespoon baking powder

- 1 cup butter, melted

Directions:

1. In a bowl, combine the cherries with the sugar, vanilla and the other ingredients, stir well and pour into a lined loaf pan, introduce the pan in the fryer and cook at 340 degrees F for 35 minutes.

2. Slice and serve.

Nutrition: calories 132, fat 6, fiber 7, carbs 11, protein 7

Cocoa and Nuts Bombs

Preparation Time: 13 minutes Servings: 12

Ingredients:

• 2 cups macadamia nuts; chopped.

• . cup cocoa powder

• 1/3 cup swerve

• 4 tbsp. coconut oil; melted

• 1 tsp. vanilla extract

Directions:

1. Take a bowl and mix all the ingredients and whisk well.

2. Shape medium balls out of this mix,place them in your air fryer and cook at 300°F for 8 minutes. Serve cold

Nutrition: Calories: 120; Fat: 12g; Fiber: 1g; Carbs: 2g; Protein: 1g

Sweet Zucchini Bread

Preparation Time: 50 minutes Servings: 12

Ingredients:

- 2 cups almond flour
- 3 eggs, whisked
- 1 cup zucchini, shredded
- . cup swerve
- . cup coconut oil; melted
- 1 tbsp. lemon zest
- 1 tsp. vanilla extract
- 2 tsp. baking powder
- 1 tsp. lemon juice
- Cooking spray

Directions:

2. Take a bowl and mix all the ingredients except the cooking spray and stir well.

3. Grease a loaf pan that fits the air fryer with the cooking spray, line with parchment paper and pour the loaf mix inside

4. Put the pan in the air fryer and cook at 330°F for 40 minutes

5. Cool down, slice and serve.

Nutrition: Calories: 143; Fat: 11g; Fiber: 1g; Carbs: 3g; Protein: 3g

Coconut

Cookies Preparation Time: 20 minutes Servings: 8

Ingredients:

• 1 . cups coconut, shredded

• 2 eggs, whisked

• 2 tbsp. Erythritol

• . tsp. almond extract

• . tsp. baking powder

Directions:

1. Take a bowl and mix all the ingredients and whisk well.

2. Scoop 8 Servings: of this mix on a baking sheet that fits the air fryer which you've lined with parchment paper.

3. Put the baking sheet in your air fryer and cook at 350°F for 15 minutes. Serve cold

Nutrition: Calories: 125; Fat: 7g; Fiber: 1g;

Carbs: 5g; Protein: 4g

Cream and Coconut Cups

Preparation Time: 15 minutes Servings: 6

Ingredients:

• 8 oz. cream cheese, soft

• 3 eggs

• 2 tbsp. butter; melted

• 3 tbsp. coconut, shredded and

unsweetened

• 4 tbsp. swerve

Directions:

1. Take a bowl and mix all the ingredients and whisk really well.

2. Divide into small ramekins, put them in the fryer and cook at 320°F and bake for 10 minutes. Serve cold

Nutrition: Calories: 164; Fat: 4g; Fiber: 2g; Carbs: 5g; Protein: 5g

Avocado Granola

Creamy Chia Seeds Pudding

Preparation Time: 35 minutes Servings: 6

Ingredients:

- 2 cups coconut cream
- . cup chia seeds
- 6 egg yolks, whisked
- 1 tbsp. ghee; melted
- 2 tbsp. stevia
- 2 tsp. cinnamon powder

Directions:

1. Take a bowl and mix all the ingredients, whisk, divide into 6 ramekins, place them all in your air fryer and cook at 340°F for 25 minutes. Cool the puddings down and serve

Nutrition: Calories: 180; Fat: 4g; Fiber: 2 carbs 5g; Protein: 7g

Cinnamon Plums

Preparation Time: 25 minutes Servings: 4

Ingredients:

• 4 plums; halved

• 3 tbsp. swerve

• 4 tbsp. butter; melted

• 2 tsp. cinnamon powder

Directions:

1. In a pan that fits your air fryer, mix the plums with the rest of the ingredients, toss, put the pan in the air fryer and cook at 300°F for 20 minutes

2. Divide into cups and serve cold.

Nutrition: Calories: 162; Fat: 3g; Fiber: 2g;

Carbs: 4g; Protein: 5g

Orangoe Cream

Preparation time: 10 minutes

Cooking time: 20 minutes

Servings: 4

Ingredients:

- 2 eggs, whisked

- 4 tablespoons sugar

- 2 cups heavy cream

- Juice of ½ orange

- ½ teaspoon orange zest, grated

Directions:

1. In a bowl, mix the eggs with the sugar and the other ingredients, whisk well, divide into 4 ramekins, place them in your air fryer and cook at 320 degrees F for 20 minutes.

2. Serve cold.

Nutrition: calories 191, fat 7, fiber 3, carbs 14, protein 4

Preparation Time: 12 minutes Servings: 6

Ingredients:

- 1 cup avocado, peeled, pitted and cubed

- . cup walnuts; chopped.

- . cup almonds; chopped.

- . cup coconut flakes

- 2 tbsp. stevia

- 2 tbsp. ghee; melted

Directions:

1. In a pan that fits your air fryer, mix all the ingredients, toss, put the pan in the fryer and cook at 320°F for 8 minutes

2. Divide into bowls and serve right away.

Nutrition: Calories: 170; Fat: 3g; Fiber: 2g; Carbs: 4g; Protein: 3g

Conclusion

Thanks for getting to the end of **Air Fryer Recipes For Beginners Super Easy And Crispy Recipes for Smart People on a Budget. A Simple Cookbook For Air Fryer Lovers**, we hope it was informative and able to provide you with all the tools you need to achieve your goals, whatever they may be.

The air fryer can take some time to get used to. It takes time to determine new habits and familiarize yourself with food replacement methods, including how to make inexpensive food tasty and satisfying.

But if you keep up, it can become a replacement lifestyle that is natural and convenient. It can also lead to some major health improvements, especially if you suffer from any condition, the keto diet proves helpful. And better health can mean fewer doctor visits and less medical bills.

CPSIA information can be obtained
at www.ICGtesting.com
Printed in the USA
BVHW091048240221
600902BV00004B/1258